Expecting Your Little Miracle

A WEEKLY
PREGNANCY DEVOTIONAL
FOR PARENTS-TO-BE

CANDACE MICHEL

ISBN 978-1-64258-525-4 (paperback)
ISBN 978-1-64258-526-1 (digital)

Christian Faith Publishing, Inc.
832 Park Avenue
Meadville, PA 16335
www.christianfaithpublishing.com

Scripture taken from the NEW AMERICAN STANDARD BIBLE®, Copyright © 1960, 1962, 1963, 1968, 1971, 1972, 1973, 1975, 1977, 1995 by The Lockman Foundation. Used by permission.

Printed in the United States of America

For Judah,
My little miracle,
and the desire of my heart.

Preface

When my husband and I planned to have a baby, the first thing that came to my mind was to pray about it. We both knew it would be a major life change, and we didn't take the responsibility lightly. It would make us parents. We would not just be the two of us any longer but three, and we would forever be responsible for this new little life that we would bring into the world. What struck me most, especially when I finally did become pregnant, was that God had blessed us with life. It is God who is the giver of life and as it says in John 14:6, "Jesus said to him, I am the way, and the truth, and the life; no one comes to the Father, but through Me." And in John 3:16, "For God so loved the world, that He gave His only begotten Son, that whoever believes in Him should not perish, but have eternal life." It is God who gives us life, both in the physical and spiritual, and life eternal for those who believe in Him. This life I carried inside of me was to come into this world, and we were responsible to raise him in the ways of the Lord, to train him up as the Bible instructs us to do. What a huge responsibility! We know that if we are believers who are saved, and followers of Christ, we are God's children, and this child was His as well. We were now given the task of caring for this new little child of God and it became very real to us that we needed help. We needed the help from God to instruct us through this journey.

So I prayed. I was reminded of Hannah from the Bible. In 1 Samuel 1:26–28 it says, And she said "Oh, my Lord! As your soul lives my Lord, I am the woman who stood here beside you, praying to the Lord. For this boy I prayed, and the Lord has given me my petition which I asked of Him. So I have also dedicated him to the Lord; as long as he lives he is dedicated to the Lord." The Lord did listen to Hannah and she had her son Samuel. It was that story that reminded me, that He also gave me what I asked of Him, and of what my heart truly desired.

As the weeks went by in that first phase of pregnancy, I desired to know what the Bible said about conception, and about starting a family, and how great of a responsibility it is to raise a child, and the instruction we are given to do so as parents.

I read books and countless articles to prepare myself, but the one thing I felt I needed most was to see what the Bible tells us. Becoming parents for the first time is such an exciting and wonderful experience, and I wanted to be prepared in both the natural as well as the supernatural.

Writing this book was in my heart since I became pregnant and had been for quite some time after. I longed for a book that would not only remind me of my physical weekly progression, but also how I could apply it to my spiritual life, to pray for the baby that was growing inside of me, to pray blessings upon it and to pray for both my husband and I. That we would learn and grow, and God would enable us to be the parents and God-centered family God designed us to be. You will see a journal page at the end of every week. Use this as a place to write down your own scriptures, thoughts or ideas, or simply a weekly note of prayer, or love for your baby. One day this could be an amazing gift to give your child. They will be blessed to know that you spent this time with them in prayer and studying God's Word. They will be able to look back one day and see and read what amazing parents you were right from the very start!

So, I pray for you and with you now, as you begin your journey. Read all you can about the books related to being pregnant and how to take care of your body. Ask your own parents and friends about their experiences, both good and bad, listen to your doctor and ask questions, and learn as much as you can. And most importantly, find some time to take care of the new spiritual journey you will embark on as new parents, and study what the Word of God says about this. Be healthy, happy, and blessed! And congratulations! You are entering the most beautiful time in your life, enjoy every moment!

God blessed them; and God said to them, "Be fruitful and multiply, and fill the earth, and subdue it; and rule over the fish of the sea and over the birds of the sky and over every living thing that moves on the earth." (Gen. 1:28)

CHAPTER I

The First Month

Weeks 1-4

Not everyone gets pregnant on the first try. We all know this. Some people do have immediate results, and others wait for years. It's a very trying journey to walk through if it's been a long road, and I understand this firsthand, having had losses of my own. It's devastating and so hard to come to grips with when you walk through this. My husband was my greatest supporter and shoulder to cry on during this period. We both felt the pain of loss, but what we always gained comfort from, was that God is our healer. We trusted in Him and remained faithful that He would provide the child we longed for if it was His perfect plan for our lives. While we tried unsuccessfully, we finally came to a point where we let it all go and gave the situation completely over to Him. I realized that my focus had become tracking every move on my pregnancy app, monitoring my ovulation schedule, and I literally lived by these things every day. I started to forget to pray and seek the Lord's help, and instead of letting my faith in God be first, I let my struggle with planning and being in control take over. The moment we realized this, and took a step back and stopped, we began to pray again. We gave it all back to God and asked Him for strength and peace, and to let Him work His will for our lives. And He did.

"Yet You are He who brought me forth from the womb; You made me trust when upon my mother's breasts. Upon You I was cast from birth; You have been my God from my mother's womb." (Ps. 22:9–10)

Week 1

So, you are either still in the process of trying to conceive, or you already have, but this first week there's technically no baby yet, however, the process has begun! It's too hard to know exactly when the egg and sperm have met. Tracking the first day of your last menstrual period is a good way to track the timing and make the start of your forty-week journey.

Continue praying for your little one. Isn't it amazing to think that God already knows if you are having a boy or girl? Who they will be, and that they are meant to be in this world for a reason. It can be a hard thing to wait for your "positive" news during these next few weeks but remember that God's timing is perfect.

What do the Scriptures say?

A Psalm of David comes to mind when I think about trusting in the Lord and waiting. Psalm 27 is a Psalm of fearless trust in God. Psalm 27:14 specifically tells us, "Wait for the Lord; be strong, and let your heart take courage; Yes, wait for the Lord."

Can you imagine a complete and fearless trust in the Lord? Read the entire Psalm through and listen to what David is saying as he cried out to the Lord, asking for help, asking to completely seek Him. This is what the Lord wants from us all the time, every day. Seek Him!

This Next Week:

Pray for a complete fearless trust in God like David did in Psalms. The Lord knows exactly what is to come even if you don't. And it's perfect. Pray on your own and together with your partner. Support each other and lean on each other. Talk about these verses and how they apply to your journey now and discuss how you can best pray for each other and encourage each other.

Notes, special thoughts, and prayers for my baby.

Week 2

*S*o, week 2 is here, and technically, you still don't have an actual baby swimming around in your belly yet, but your body is still working overtime to make sure that the ovulation cycle is happening, and the perfect little egg (or eggs, maybe it's twins!) is gearing up for its big moment when that one lucky sperm finally reaches it and the two become one. The miracle is just about to begin!

Isn't it truly amazing how our bodies work? That right now, you still haven't technically conceived yet, but in only thirty-eight short weeks (believe me, they go by very quickly!) you will be holding your baby in your arms. If that's not the work of the Lord, and a complete miracle, I don't know what is!

What do the Scriptures say?

The verse in Jeremiah 1:5 says to us, "Before I formed you in the womb I knew you, And before you were born I consecrated you; I have appointed you a prophet to the nations."

The Lord came to Jeremiah and spoke those words to him, and if you read the entire chapter you will hear the Lord encourage Jeremiah when he questions himself and his youth. This is another example of trusting in the Lord. He has known us even before we were formed, and He loved us then and still loves us now. Our best interest is always in His heart and we are reminded of this constantly throughout the Bible.

The other scripture that I felt was important to me at this time was a prayer of thanksgiving. Thanking God for what He was yet to do. Psalm 100 is a Psalm where all men are exhorted to praise God! The entire chapter reads:

> "Shout joyfully to the Lord, all the earth. Serve the Lord with gladness; Come before Him with joyful singing. Know that the Lord Himself is

God; It is He who has made us, and not we ourselves; We are His people and the sheep of His pasture. Enter His gates with thanksgiving, and His courts with praise. Give thanks to Him; bless His name. For the Lord is good; His lovingkindness is everlasting, and His faithfulness to all generations."

This Next Week:

Pray and praise God for what He has done, what He is doing, and what He will do! God is so good and so faithful. Continue to pray on your own, and with your partner as Psalm 100 tells us to!

Notes, special thoughts, and prayers for my baby.

Week 3

Okay, are you ready for it? You have conceived! Praise the Lord, the miracle He has created inside of you has now begun to take shape! As soon as the sperm met the egg, the fertilized cell then starts dividing over and over into an itty-bitty ball of cells now headed to your uterus to get nice and cozy for the next thirty-seven weeks.

Although you may not be feeling the effects quite yet, talk to your doctor and make sure you are taking care of your body and doing all that is needed to stay healthy for yourself and your baby. It may be a good time for you and your partner to get on a good clean healthy eating menu and lifestyle together. Believe me, when baby actually arrives, you'll feel better, have more energy for long days and nights, and you'll feel so much better overall!

What do the Scriptures say?

We should always be healthy and respect our bodies, especially now at such an important time, but also remember that our bodies are the Lord's. 1 Corinthians 6:19–20 tell us, "Or do you not know that your body is a temple of the Holy Spirit who is in you, whom you have from God, and that you are not your own? For you have been bought with a price: therefore, glorify God in your body."

It's pretty clear we are instructed to take care of ourselves. Would you invite someone of high importance over to your home if it was a messy disaster? Probably not. So, think of it the same way with your body. Your body is a temple and the Lord lives inside of you. Take care of that home He dwells in. Inside and out.

This Next Week:

If you haven't done so already, begin a healthier living routine in your home for you and your partner. Within the guidelines of your doctor, begin a healthy meal plan, exercise, and even take the time to rest and create a stress-free environment for yourself. Pick out a time with your partner that works for you both to pray together, read the Bible together, study through this book, or any other devotional book. Along with your prayer and study routine, you may want to develop a diary of verses and topics you studied. Even if it's just a quick note-taking of specific verses you both read. It's something you can look back on and pass on to your child one day. To give them the gift of knowing that they were loved and prayed for and thought of the moment they were conceived!

Notes, special thoughts, and prayers for my baby.

Week 4

Okay, so it gets more exciting now as the weeks progress. Your baby is in the embryo stage and is all curled up and snuggly in your uterus where it will stay until it comes into the world. Baby is about the size of a poppy seed right now. The miraculous part of it all is that it's developing so quickly. The amniotic sac is forming; the yolk sac is forming; and each layer of the embryo is beginning to grow into specialized parts of the body. Wow! And it's so small!

What do the Scripture say?

God knows everything about us. Whether it's how the layers of the embryo are forming into parts of the body, or simply what we might be thinking this very moment, God knows. And He cares. He cares about every detail of our lives.

We can be reminded of this in Psalm 139. The chapter written by David reads of God's omnipresence and omniscience. Verses 13–16 read, "For Thou didst form my inward parts; Thou didst weave me in my mother's womb. I will give thanks to Thee, for I am fearfully and wonderfully made; Wonderful are Thy works, and my soul knows it very well. My frame was not hidden from Thee, when I was made in secret, and skillfully wrought in the depths of the earth. Thine eyes have seen my unformed substance; and in Thy book they were all written, the days that were ordained for me, when as yet there was not one of them."

Is that not amazing? God is only just forming this tiny baby in your body, yet He knows every day that boy or girl will spend on earth and every move they will make. It is all ordained, yet they are still to come.

This Next Week:

This Scripture should be a prayerful reminder to you that you are now parents and this baby inside of you is being fearfully and wonderfully made by the Lord who already has a perfect plan for this tiny person. Make it a priority to pray that His will may be done in your child's life. Pray that you will raise them up to know and serve the Lord all the days of their lives. We, as parents, are responsible for this. Make this prayer a priority now, and for the rest of your lives.

Notes, special thoughts, and prayers for my baby.

_____
_____
_____
_____
_____
_____
_____
_____
_____
_____
_____
_____
_____
_____
_____
_____
_____
_____
_____
_____
_____
_____
_____
_____

CHAPTER 2

The Second Month

Weeks 5–8

Like myself, and most others, you are probably only confirming the positive pregnancy news in the next couple of weeks. I was about five weeks along when I found out I was pregnant. Whether you are taking the store-bought home tests, or going straight to your doctor for blood tests, you are going to get that official positive reading. I remember taking photos of my two pink lines! It was such an exciting feeling. At first, I couldn't help but wonder if my eyes were crossed, or was I really seeing what I thought I saw! Either way, this is such a happy time for you and your partner. A time of celebration and such joy. Make sure to take the time to talk to your partner about how long you want to keep your little secret, or perhaps you want to go online and immediately tell the world. It's your joy, and you are entitled to deliver that happy news in your time, the way you want to. Enjoy it!

By this time, you are most likely feeling those first telltale signs of body changes, mood changes, and feeling strange things! Everyone is different. Don't compare or worry if your friends are saying they all got morning sickness. You may not, and if you don't, lucky you! We all have different pregnancies, and it's your own special journey. Embrace these changes. Some of them may not be pleasant, but many are. I personally enjoyed the entire nine months of being pregnant. I was very blessed to have had minimal negative effects and truly enjoyed it.

In the next few weeks we will read more about what the Bible says to us about how the Lord is righteous and near to those who love Him. All of our cares and worries are also His. Including pregnancy! Why not pray and ask God for a healthy, stress-free, and enjoyable pregnancy? I constantly thanked the Lord for giving me this blessing and journey and simply asked for an easy and healthy pregnancy. Yes, I had a few moments, but I believe He answered my simple prayers and gave me a very enjoyable nine months. I honestly had never felt so alive, healthy, and beautiful until then, ever.

Start having a positive attitude about all your new feelings and changes, and cast your cares upon Him, and begin rejoicing in this beautiful journey He designed your body to be on!

Week 5

Baby looks like a tiny little tadpole. How adorable is that? It is about the size of an orange seed, and the most amazing part is that the heart is beginning to take shape and form and be operational. So yes, you have a living being inside of you. What a perfect miracle God is creating! I remember this moment so well. Knowing that inside of me, were a total of two heartbeats. I thought about it all of the time. I had never felt so alive. I thought a lot about my own heart. How was I living? Was my heart and life a reflection of God? And now that I carried this tiny little baby inside of me, with a perfect beating heart of its own, I knew I needed to refocus some of my priorities and begin living differently. It's like the saying "Good stuff in, good stuff out." I really believe that still today. I needed to live my life in a way where I was an example of Christ, and my heart would show the love of the Lord. That my baby, from the first heartbeat, would feel the love of God working through me and living inside of me and it would know it was safe and loved and held.

What do the Scriptures say?

I remember back in Sunday school, we memorized the Beatitudes in Matthew 5:1–10. I thought of this Scripture early in my pregnancy and when I went to open my Bible to this passage, it was not only highlighted, but starred! I could tell from my slightly messy notes that it had been many years since I had made those highlights and it made me glad. Some Scripture stays with you and strengthens you throughout your life. This was one of mine.

Verse 8 simply says, "Blessed are the pure in heart, for they shall see God." This verse brings tears to my eyes almost every time I read it. It was my fervent prayer to be pure in heart. For my baby, for myself, and mostly, because one day, I believe I *shall* see God. I believe it with all of my heart. It was now my desire to live better than I ever had in my life because it was now my responsibility to teach my child to be pure in heart also.

This Next Week:

Read the Beatitudes from the Lord's Sermon on the Mount in Matthew. Sit down and pray with your partner, and be honest about the things in each of your lives that you can change. We are all sinners and we must all ask for forgiveness, but it should be the constant desire of your heart to want to change, to be like Him. You will be examples to your child and having a pure, clean heart for God should be taught and shown from day one.

Notes, special thoughts, and prayers for my baby.

Week 6

our baby's legs are being formed in a bent shape! If your baby is only about a quarter of an inch "tall," imagine how tiny that actually is. Seriously, look at your leg right now, then go get a measuring tape to actually see how small a quarter of an inch is, and then imagine the tiniest little leg you've ever seen. Okay, but even more than that, your baby's jaws, cheeks, chin, and indentations for ears are forming. Tiny little black eye dots are appearing and the tiniest little bump of a nose is also present. I'm honestly smiling from ear to ear as I think about this because obviously *your* baby is the cutest little baby in the world already (it's okay to think that, we all do it), and when everything is super tiny and miniature, well, come on! You couldn't find a onesie small enough. I bet you could find something online.

Most mamas are making their first doctor's visits for prenatal care, and understanding what the next seven and a half months of care will look like. My husband and I enjoyed my OB/GYN doctor very much and felt very comfortable. The one thing, however, that I started picking up on was all of the references to special tests, what is looked for in ultrasounds and why, how they check for issues with baby and you . . . they want to keep you safe and healthy! Listen to your doctor! I admit though, that the more I learned and read, the more fearful I became at times. I let my trust in God take a seat in my doctor's waiting room, and I would walk in alone. How stupid of me. I let doubt creep into my mind and it would wander. I constantly had to kick myself and remind myself to stop. The first thing I needed to do was pray and ask for peace at these appointments. I would not let the fear of something being wrong with my baby to come over me. I would trust in God for a healthy pregnancy. God's will would be done in my life and however it turned out, I would trust and believe that He had the *best* for me.

What do the Scriptures say?

"Trust in the Lord with all your heart, and do not lean on your own understanding." (Prov. 3:5)

"And now, oh Lord God, Thou are God, and Thy words are truth, and Thou hast promised this good thing to Thy servant." (2 Sam. 7:28)

"Behold, God is my salvation, I will trust and not be afraid; for the Lord God is my strength and song, and He has become my salvation." (Isa. 12:2)

This Next Week:

I would encourage you all this week to pray with your partner to lean not on your own understanding but to begin to wholly and completely trust in God. Whether it be prenatal appointments you will be starting, or any other new or standing issues in your life. Take the time to go through the Bible and look for verses about trust and strength. The Bible is full of encouragement and expressions of thanksgiving on this subject. A solid trust in the Lord brings so much peace and confidence and assuredness to our lives. Even for a doctor visit!

Notes, special thoughts, and prayers for my baby.

_____
_____
_____
_____
_____
_____
_____
_____
_____
_____
_____
_____
_____
_____
_____
_____
_____
_____
_____
_____
_____
_____
_____

Week 7

Your baby is the size of a blueberry! And depending on how you are feeling right now, that may have just made you hungry. It's okay, go ahead and get a snack. Your baby is growing at such a fast pace right now. The mouth and tongue are forming, and I think one of the most amazing things is that the kidneys are actually in place and they are ready to start working! Those are some of the tiniest little working organs I have ever heard of.

I especially love that baby's mouth is forming. Every time I see my son first thing in the morning, he usually has a smile on those little lips and if you want to have your heart melt, literally every day, just wait until your baby smiles at you. They are the most kissable, sweetest little lips I've ever seen. And the giggles and coos that your baby will one day make. The sweetest sounds you have ever heard. Be still my heart!

The Bible talks very specifically about the words we speak from our mouths. Right now your baby may not be able to open their mouth or speak, but you can, and not only can your baby hear what you say, so does everyone around you, most of all, the Lord.

What do the Scriptures say?

In Ephesians 4:29 the Bible says, "Let no unwholesome word proceed from your mouth, but only such a word as is good for edification according to the need of the moment, that it may give grace to those who hear."

Oh, how I wish I could go back in time and take back things I have said to people, or about people behind their backs, or even lies I have told. We all have moments like these, but thankfully Jesus came to die for our sins so we may be saved. I know I am forgiven when I ask Him and have forgiven those who have also sinned against me.

When I was pregnant, I became so aware of certain language I used, music I listened to, things I said, as well as conversations with others that I knew I should not be part of. We should always be conscious of these things, but now I wanted to protect my pure little baby. I made an effort to watch my words. To think carefully before I spoke. My voice was the voice my baby would hear the most. I needed those words that came from my mouth to be positive. I also needed to speak of the Lord, sing praises to Him, and speak words of life.

Proverbs 18:21 says, "Death and life are in the power of the tongue, and those who love it will eat its fruit."

This Next Week:

Make it a point for both you and your partner to pay close attention to what you speak from your mouth. What you say is very powerful. Let those words be full of life to your little one from now on. Pray together, out loud so your baby can hear you! Even in your car, be careful of what you are listening to. Your baby will hear it too. Sing songs of praise that will be uplifting. It is another example of "Good stuff in, good stuff out!"

Notes, special thoughts, and prayers for my baby.

_____
_____
_____
_____
_____
_____
_____
_____
_____
_____
_____
_____
_____
_____
_____
_____
_____
_____
_____
_____
_____
_____
_____
_____
_____

Week 8

Baby this week is bigger still, about the size of a raspberry and growing nonstop. One of the magical little things happening is that baby is actually starting to twitch, and move a little bit. You could never feel this movement at this stage, but it's happening! Its heart rate is rapidly beating at about twice the speed of your own, and more and more its face and body is really taking shape.

Knowing that your little one is actually moving inside of you is a pretty miraculous thing, isn't it? It seems to bring on a whole new aspect of being alive somehow. From this moment on, your baby will not stop moving either. For the rest of its life inside of you and then the moment it enters our world, your baby will be alive and moving. Learning new things, copying every move you make, following you around, learning to crawl and walk, and then eventually as they become older, they will use their hands and bodies to work, to show love, and if we have taught our children correctly, they will use their body to praise God. They will lift their hands to the heavens in prayer and song, and glorify the Lord. In all things, to be alive in Christ!

What do the Scriptures say?

Ephesians 2:10 says, "For we are His workmanship, created in Christ Jesus for good works, which God prepared beforehand, that we should walk in them."

Right now God is creating your tiny baby in His own image, and that he or she would walk in His ways, doing good works and living for the Lord. That is what we were all created to do.

This Next Week:

Pray with your partner this week for your baby, that while God is continuing to create this little one, that you are already praying for its walk with the Lord. You will be their parents, and responsible for training them up in the ways of the Lord. Seek the Lord for guidance and the right ways to lead your child. If we are His workmanship, we need to be a constant example of this to our children and train them to do the same.

Notes, special thoughts, and prayers for my baby.

_____
_____
_____
_____
_____
_____
_____
_____
_____
_____
_____
_____
_____
_____
_____
_____
_____
_____
_____
_____
_____
_____
_____

CHAPTER 3

The Third Month

Weeks 9–13

I think there's a sense of relief as you reach the last couple of weeks in the first trimester. There is a normal sense of finally being able to relax as that first three months has come and gone and you know that baby has overcome one of the more sensitive times of pregnancy and if you haven't told the world yet that you are pregnant, I'm sure you are just about to—if it's not starting to show yet!

Because I had walked through two miscarriages before having my son, this was definitely a big milestone for me. My pregnancy with my son was different though somehow. From the moment I found out I was pregnant, I knew that it was going to be all right. I had a sense of peace I will never be able to fully explain to anyone. I literally felt warm. I felt as though the Lord had wrapped me in His arms and held me and told me not to worry or fear, but to trust Him as I had been. This feeling carried on with me through the entire nine months. Yes, I still had troubling thoughts at times and natural feelings of fear, but ultimately I knew I was going to carry this baby full term with a clean bill of health.

My trust in the Lord at this point in my life was at the highest and purest it had ever been in my life, which for me translated into peace. A peace that only can come from the Lord himself. We all pray for peace for ourselves, or maybe a loved one when they are going through a hard time, but it was truly the first time in my life I can say I felt it wash over me.

I would encourage you to read the entirety of Psalm 119 (it's long, but such a beautifully written meditation and prayer relating to the law of God). The one verse I will point out is Psalm 119:165, "Those who love Thy law have great peace, and nothing causes them to stumble."

If you are still worried or feeling nervous, it is totally normal, especially if this is your first pregnancy, but remember that you are not alone and God is right there with you. He knows your thoughts and feelings, and all you need to do is ask Him to take all of your worry from you and grant you a sense of peace.

The Lord himself says in John 14:27, "Peace I leave with you; My peace I give to you; not as the world gives, do I give to you. Let not your heart be troubled, nor let it be fearful."

Week 9

*Y*our baby, which by most health professionals, is now called a fetus (but come on, let's just keep calling it baby, right?), and is about an inch long. Maybe the size of an olive or a grape. It's developing muscle and it is allowing baby to move its tiny little arms and legs better. We still won't feel anything for at least another month or so, but rest assured that the little guy is practicing his kickboxing!

For some people, you may be able to hear the heartbeat if you have a doctor appointment coming up. Don't worry if you can't hear it the first time. Your doctor will still be able to see baby's heart on the monitor. It will happen!

I will tell you that this appointment is sure to make your own heart beat faster and perhaps grow a little bigger. It will be the first sound you ever hear from your baby. I totally cried! I had my husband take a video of the whole event . . . something you might want to consider if you want to record it and listen to it over and over like I did!

What do the Scriptures say?

I still remember driving home from that appointment when I heard my son's heartbeat for the first time. In my head was a (very old) chorus that we used to sing in church when I was growing up. The chorus is based on a verse from Psalm 51:10, "Create in me a clean heart, O God, and renew a steadfast spirit within me."

I thought about the fact that my baby had a pure and clean heart. It knows nothing of the world and of sin and it is still pure and being created in God's image. This is the kind of heart we should all desire.

This Next Week:

Psalm 51 is a sinner's prayer for pardon. Read through the entire chapter with your partner. To be pure of heart in our own personal lives and then as parents, is an essential prayer we all must pray for and then strive to live by.

Notes, special thoughts, and prayers for my baby.

_____
_____
_____
_____
_____
_____
_____
_____
_____
_____
_____
_____
_____
_____
_____
_____
_____
_____
_____
_____
_____
_____
_____

Week 10

So another half an inch has been added to your baby's height this week! Now at a whopping one and a half inches tall, baby is about as big as a prune now! Elbows are working and the tiny little buds that will be your baby's teeth are actually forming under its itty-bitty little gums. Seriously, people, how adorable is that? But my favorite part is probably that those little legs are beginning to develop knees and ankles. The tiny little joints that will allow your child to walk and to run!

I'm sure you are reading books and have some sort of online app that gives you the daily play by play on your baby's development, but with each passing week, aren't you totally amazed at how quickly your baby actually is growing and developing these functions, still at such a small size? I'm still constantly amazed by the miracle of life that God allows us to grow in our bodies. Talk about a perfectly designed plan!

I can't help but think about legs and feet, and walking this week. Your baby will one day get up on his or her feet, and take their first steps, and you will run and grab for your cell phone to get it on video and take pictures so you can immediately send it to your own parents and share it on social media. But it's totally okay. You will be proud parents and you should be. We all know that our own children are perfect and everything they do is amazing!

But back to our feet . . .

What do the Scriptures say?

Our feet can direct many paths in our lives. They can take us into very terrible places, or we can direct them on the path that God wants us to walk down. If you once again go to Psalm 119, verse 105 says, "Thy word is a lamp unto my feet, and a light unto my path."

This verse has always been a very constant reminder for me through my entire life. Am I following the path that God has lit up for me? Or am I blindly fumbling through the darkness, trying to feel my way around and make it through on my own?

This Next Week:

God has given this baby to you as a part of your path in life and a part of God's plan for you. Pray together with your partner about your paths in your own lives as well as together. It's no longer just the two of you walking any longer. Your baby will follow in your footsteps. Pray that you will be leading them down the right path and that you will be examples in the places you go, the things you see, and that you will "walk the walk, and not just talk the talk." Show them the way!

Notes, special thoughts, and prayers for my baby.

Week 11

We are right at about two inches this week! Baby's body is slowly straightening out, hair follicles are forming, as well as the fingernail and toenail beds. Your baby's gender is being determined as well. If you are having a girl, ovaries are slowly developing. Isn't it just incredible to think of this tiny human, only two inches long, but having all those tiny features already formed and taking shape? Even its face is taking on many of its final shapes. If you aren't feeling very tired on a constant basis yet, then you are very blessed—your body is working overtime!

I really began to think about gender at this point in my own pregnancy. My husband and I decided not to find out the gender until the delivery, and it was very hard not to know! I completely understand why you would want to. That was a long nine months to wait, but I have to tell you, as an adult, in life, I don't think there are any truly great surprises left for us. Big ones, I mean. We both decided that this was one thing that we had zero control over in our lives, and no matter if it was a boy or girl, that baby was meant to be born for a reason. It was already in God's plan. So we decided to hold out.

As we think of gender roles as parents, we definitely do play very different roles in our families. Every family is built differently, but you need to discuss now with your partner what sort of duties or roles you will want to have once the baby arrives. What sort of example will you be setting? Will you both be working? Will you share the nighttime responsibilities together? Will you need to adjust the household duties and share the load of chores?

Whether you are traditional in your roles or not, you need to think about this now. Talk to your friends and family about how they handled it, and then discuss together for how you want to handle your own situation. Don't wait until you have your baby home and chaos has already begun. It's going to take some team work and some pretty big adjustments. Both of you need to know what you expect from each other. Communicate now, not at three in the morning the first week home!

What do the Scriptures say?

The Bible tells us of many instances where there are very different roles that male and females play. Singularly, and together as a couple. Many people have many different thoughts and feelings about gender roles throughout the Bible, but what I personally see are many instances where God makes it very clear in favor of both the man and woman. Ephesians 5 speaks very clearly about being imitators of God, having a marriage like Christ and the church, and family relationships. For example, in verse 22 and 23 it reads, "Wives, be subject to your own husbands, as to the Lord. For the husband is the head of the wives as Christ also is the head of the church." I know many women find this hard to accept in today's world, but keep reading . . . in verse 25 it then goes on to say, "Husbands, love your wives, just as Christ loved the church and gave Himself up for her."

It is not stating that the wife is a slave. It is calling a wife to honor and respect her husband, giving him charge of the household. But not as a dictator. No. Husbands are to love their wives as Christ loved the church. Do you know how much love, adoration, respect, and honor that commandment holds?

Another verse that I find very thoughtful on this subject comes from 1 Corinthians 11:12. It reads, "For as the woman originates from the man, so also the man has his birth through the woman; and all things originate from God."

This Next Week:

We need to respect each other at all times, show love and honor, and make sure that this is outwardly shown in your home. Whether you are having a girl or a boy, you will be raising that little person in a way where you will be showing them how to treat their spouse one day. Make sure that it is in a Godly, honorable way. A way that has been commanded of us, in our God-centered marriages. Raise them to see this on a daily basis.

Pray this week that you and your partner will strive to be good partners for each other now and in the future for your children. Your family dynamic will hinge on how your relationships unfolds in your home. Make sure you are strong in Christ and centered in your marriage.

Notes, special thoughts, and prayers for my baby.

Week 12

Your baby is about the size of a plum! The development of baby is still in full gear as well. Most of his or her systems are formed but more is still to come. One thing I find so fascinating right now is that your baby is producing hormones of its own and there are white blood cells being made to help fight off germs and diseases! All in such a tiny little person!

While your baby is safely tucked inside your womb, you are able to protect them from colds and nasty bugs that we all inevitably get from time to time. Hopefully you don't have to bear a cold while you are pregnant!

Hopefully you are taking good care of yourself and feeling well. Most people seem to get over morning sickness and major fatigue at this point. We all experience things differently, so again, never compare or let anyone tell you how it should be. Whether good or bad, embrace it!

I believe that doing our part in maintaining a healthy pregnancy is key. The foods we eat, listening to your doctor, being active, living a clean life. But also, our minds need to be clean and we need to remain healthy in our spirits as well.

What do the Scriptures say?

I had a very easy pregnancy. I may be "lucky" as I've been told many times, but more than luck, I believe in the power of prayer. I prayed every day for a safe day for my baby and I. I went for nine months without a cold. I had no serious side effects. I truly believed that God would deliver me from any sickness or disease and that my nine months would be enjoyable. I believed it and I prayed for it.

One verse that is an older worship song from church is from Isaiah 40: 29–31, "He gives strength to the weary, and to him who lacks might He increases power. Though youths grow weary and tired, and vigorous young men stumble badly, yet those who wait for the Lord will gain new strength; they will mount up with wings like eagles, they will run and not get tired, they will walk and not become weary."

Why can't you ask for renewed strength? If you are feeling tired or unwell or just want an extra boost, ask Him. The Word of God is full of promises for us. As He is creating those special blood cells in your baby to protect it, why not ask Him to renew the cells you already have!

This Next Week:

Continue as partners to pray daily for strength, health, and wellness for you and for your baby, so this can be the beautiful experience it is designed to be.

Notes, special thoughts, and
prayers for my baby.

Week 13

Well, you are officially at the end of your first trimester, it's a big milestone! The next six months are going to fly by just as fast! Your baby in just one week has grown so much. Baby is about three inches long, and will continue to grow overtime. The intestines are fixing themselves into their permanent position in the abdomen and maybe most exciting, the vocal cords are developing!

The first thing you will hear from your baby is their cry, and I assure you it's the sweetest sound you will ever hear. It made me cry when I heard my son cry out for the first time. It's that "everything is going to be okay" kind of sound.

Your baby is going to have their own individual sounding voice—maybe high, maybe low. Maybe they will become a great singer. Whatever tone comes out, it will be your favorite sound, I'm sure.

It makes me think about what we use our voices for. We've read about "good things in, good things out," that it's very important for what we say and hear to be good and pure, especially in front of our little ones. But our voices were also designed for praise and worship. How often do we use those strong vocal cords to really cry out to the Lord in worship and prayer?

What do the Scriptures say?

If you want to read about praise, open your Bible to Psalm 100:1–2 says, "Shout joyfully to the Lord, all the earth. Serve the Lord with gladness. Come before Him with singing."

Psalm 104:33 says, "I will sing to the Lord as long as I live; I will sing praise to my God while I have my being."

One thing you can see is that there's no ending to these statements. We are to praise God all our lives, and do it joyfully.

This Next Week:

I know we can't all spontaneously start singing at our office or in the middle of the grocery store, but we can always be thinking about it. Let your singing be in the car, at home while doing chores, in church, and remember how much you have to be joyful for. You have a perfect baby inside of you. Teach it to have a joyful heart, full of praise. Remember that your baby can hear you. Let it hear songs and prayers to the One who made you!

Notes, special thoughts, and prayers for my baby.

CHAPTER 4

The Fourth Month

Weeks 14–17

Starting the second trimester is usually the beginning of a really exciting time for most women. Most of your family and friends know you are expecting, and the excitement is everywhere. There's a very good chance you are starting to "show" and not just look like you gained a few extra pounds! You may find it easier on a day-to-day basis to feel somewhat normal. Hopefully any signs of nausea or sickness you may have had in the beginning have lessened. These next three months will most likely be the easiest of your pregnancy.

Throughout my pregnancy I was thankful. I remember praying a prayer of thanks to the Lord daily for the gift He had given us. I was constantly moved to tears with thankfulness and happiness. I hope you are feeling fantastic and remember to thank the Lord daily for that. Thank Him for all things, for all that you have and all that you are given. Be thankful!

"Let the peace of Christ rule in your hearts, to which indeed you were called in one body; and be thankful. Let the word of Christ richly dwell within you, with one another with psalms and hymns and spiritual songs, singing with thankfulness in your hearts to God. And whatever you do in word or deed, do all in the name of the Lord Jesus, giving thanks through Him to God the Father." (Col. 5: 15–17)

Week 14

This week your baby is about the size of your clenched fist. Talk about fast growth! There is also a good chance that your baby may be sprouting its first few hairs on the top of his head. I've always found it funny how some babies come out completely bald (like I did!) and then some come out with a full head of hair thicker than an adult.

It's amazing to think that God knows how that little person is going to look, exactly how many hairs they will have on their head, and that the features that are growing and forming are exactly perfect in His image.

This is once again a constant reminder to us to trust in Him. He knows everything about you, and always has from the time of conception and even before. It is not by chance we are here, and it is not by chance your baby is here now too. Your baby has a destiny and a path set out for them, and yet they have not even taken their first breath. What an amazing thought. The Lord has worked out every detail according to His plan, so we must have faith in Him that He will surely lead us if we are willing to listen and follow.

What do the Scriptures say?

In Luke 12:7 is says, "Indeed, the very hairs of your head are all numbered. Do not fear; you are of more value than many sparrows."

God really does know, see, and care about even the smallest details of our lives, including how many hairs we have on our head! It's almost too hard to comprehend the love He has for us. You will love your baby the moment you set your eyes on them. It will be a love you have never experienced before. Remember that moment when it comes, and remember that God loves you even more. He loves your baby even more. Jesus died on the cross for your baby as well, that their sins may be forgiven. There truly is no greater gift!

This Next Week:

Pray, especially for your little one, that they will come to know Christ, and through your teachings as parents, learn the love that God has for them and that He sent His Son to die for their sins and salvation. Pray that you will be the example they need to learn to understand this and live it throughout their lives. Let them know just how loved they are by you, but especially by the One who created them.

*Notes, special thoughts, and
prayers for my baby.*

_____
_____
_____
_____
_____
_____
_____
_____
_____
_____
_____
_____
_____
_____
_____
_____
_____
_____
_____
_____
_____
_____
_____
_____
_____
_____
_____

Week 15

*Y*our baby most likely has the final positioning of their ears set this week, and the eyes are moving from the sides of the face to the front. It has good coordination already and is moving its teeny tiny little fingers and toes, and may even be sucking on its thumb! Oh my, how adorable! Baby can also make sucking and breathing movements now. Sure, it is not breathing air, but it's all in preparation for the big day when it takes its first breath. You most likely cannot feel any of these movements yet as baby is still quite small, but rest assured, it's working out!

It's truly amazing to think that even in the womb, a baby is instinctively given the sensations to breathe and move.

What do the Scriptures say?

God is the giver of life, in all of us. In the very beginning, God the Creator breathed His breath of life into all of creation, including man.

Genesis 2:7 says, "Then the Lord God formed man of dust from the ground, and breathed into his nostrils the breath of life; and man became a living being."

Job 12:10 says, "In whose hand is the life of every living thing. And the breath of all mankind?"

We can read in the Bible and know for certain that God Himself has formed man and breathed life into him, so he can live. Not just Adam, but *every* living thing. The breath of *all* mankind. It is through Him that we can live.

And what should we be doing with the breath that God has breathed into us? The very last verse in the book of Psalm is very clear. Psalm 150 is a Psalm of praise and verse 6 says, "Let everything that has breath, praise the Lord. Praise the Lord."

This Next Week:

Praise God this week in all you do. For with every single breath you take, it is God that has breathed that life into you and your baby as well. We live because He has given us life. Use the breath He's given you and praise Him with it. That's why He created us, to praise Him!

Notes, special thoughts, and prayers for my baby.

_____

_____

_____

_____

_____

_____

_____

_____

_____

_____

_____

_____

_____

_____

_____

_____

_____

_____

_____

_____

_____

_____

_____

_____

Week 16

*Y*our baby's eyes have now found their place, complete with adorable little eyebrows and the most thick, long fluttery eyelashes you will probably ever see. Just wait until they look up at you and melt your heart! Their little eyes have started to move as well. They can move from side to side and can see light through their eyelids, although still sealed.

Our eyes are such an important sense to us, aren't they? They allow us to see the beauty all around us, look into the eyes of the ones we love, shed tears of happiness or sadness, and they really are windows to a soul. I know I can look into the eyes of my husband and know if he is happy or sad. We can speak volumes just by looking at someone with our eyes.

What we see with our eyes can be beautiful, but we also know that it can be ugly and we can't "un-see" terrible things once we have beheld them. Only we know, ourselves, what we have seen in our lives, whether on purpose or not, and there may be times we do not have control over that, but many times we do.

Are we shielding ourselves from going places where we may see things that are sinful and could be of an addictive or dangerous nature? Watching movies or shows that burn evil images into our brains that make us have nightmares? Why do we as humans constantly seek out these terrible images to scar ourselves with? We then need to consider what we want our children to see! Oh, how we need to protect them more than ever from the much too easily accessed media that is everywhere today.

What do the Scriptures say?

Nobody but us can know what we've seen and hold secret in our hearts, except God. Proverbs 15:3 reminds us "The eyes of the Lord are in every place, watching the evil and the good." God sees all we do. We should be feeling a lot more shame than we probably do if we would remember this simple verse.

This Next Week:

Take stock of what your habits are around what you are seeing and viewing on a regular basis. Make changes now. For yourselves, and to strengthen and purify your relationship with the Lord, and also to get into clean habits for what your children will eventually see. Their tiny eyes will look to you for all the answers to life. They will imitate you, and follow everything you do. Make sure to always remember that they are watching you. You want to make sure those actions they copy are good ones. Above all, pray for strength from the Lord that He will help you to make the changes you know you may need to make for your own lives. Keep that old little Sunday school song in the back of your head "Be careful little eyes what you see!"

*Notes, special thoughts, and
prayers for my baby.*

_____
_____
_____
_____
_____
_____
_____
_____
_____
_____
_____
_____
_____
_____
_____
_____
_____
_____
_____
_____
_____
_____
_____
_____
_____

Week 17

*Y*our little babe is about the size of your palm now, and although quite skinny still, it is slowly starting to put on some fat. Although you may be feeling like you don't want to put any more weight on yourself, it's all a good thing! You are so beautiful! I really believe that a pregnant woman is absolutely gorgeous. It's one of the most radiant and beautiful times of life you can ever go through. Enjoy the few extra pounds!

Also being regulated is the heart rate. Close to double the rate of an adult heart rate, your baby's heart is probably coming in at right around 140–150 beats per minute.

We have already looked into God's Word regarding our hearts, but there's so much the Bible says about this, about protecting our hearts, keeping them clean and pure. God also speaks of not letting our hearts be troubled, and to trust in Him. Even through a pregnancy we can apply this. It's natural to have moments of fear and uncertainty in any new experience, but we must always remember to trust in God and know that His best is being worked out on our behalf!

What do the Scriptures say?

Jesus needed to comfort His disciples at times as well! As humans, it is natural to worry and feel scared or doubtful but the Scriptures are a perfect reminder of God's gentleness and comfort for us. In John 14:1–2 the Lord says to His disciples, "Let not your heart be troubled; believe in God, believe also in Me. In My Father's house are many dwelling places; if it were not so, I would have told you; for I go to prepare a place for you."

This Next Week:

The Lord knows your heart better than anyone, and He knows your baby's heart too. His best interests are always right there waiting for you. Seek the Lord about what is on your heart today. No burden is too small or too heavy for Him.

Notes, special thoughts, and prayers for my baby.

_____
_____
_____
_____
_____
_____
_____
_____
_____
_____
_____
_____
_____
_____
_____
_____
_____
_____
_____
_____
_____
_____
_____
_____
_____

CHAPTER 5

The Fifth Month

Weeks 18–22

Did you know that for most women, this is the month that you will finally feel your baby move? I remember very well the moment it happened for me. I was in my twenty-first week, and I had gone to bed to read for the night. I was lying there very still and out of nowhere, a huge kick jolted me on my right side. I sat straight up and couldn't believe the feeling! I went out to excitedly tell my husband and for some reason I wept.

Although my pregnancy had been very real to me the whole time, it was an obvious sign of life. A tangible sign that my baby was really in there and that this tiny person was truly inside of me.

It made me think about my faith in the Lord. We who believe in Him, know that although we may not see Him, we can feel Him. We can see the Lord in creation, in weather, in the sign and promise that the rainbow will bring us when it has just rained, but we cannot literally look and see the face of God. We instead put our faith in Him and know He is real because of the Holy Spirit moving through us. Through miracles and answered prayers, and the joy and wondrous feeling we have when we have been saved and sanctified through Jesus Christ our Lord and Savior.

I know my Redeemer lives and I can feel Him in my life. And if I am willing, and listen very carefully, I know I can often hear Him speak if my heart is open and wanting to hear what He has to say to me.

It may be hard for many to believe in something they cannot see, but just as I could not see my baby inside of my womb, I knew he was there because I could feel him, and my faith in the amazing miracle that God was creating inside of me was the greatest proof of all.

Week 18

As your baby is still growing and moving more and more with kicks and punches, twists and rolls, if you haven't already felt them, you will very soon. And get ready for it—it is a little strange! I loved feeling my son move inside of me, but there were times when honestly, it just felt plain weird!

A really special and unique development this week is that baby has developed fingerprints on its fingertips and toes! We all know that this is one of the things that makes us truly unique from one another and make us, us!

God has used His own hands and fingers to create the heavens and the earth, and He has fashioned us in His own image.

What do the Scriptures say?

In Psalm 8:1–3 the Psalmist David sings, "O Lord, our Lord, how majestic is Thy name in all the earth, Who hast displayed Thy splendor above the heavens! From the mouth of infants and nursing babes Thou hast established strength, because of Thine adversaries, to make the enemy and the revengeful cease. When I consider Thy heavens, the work of Thy fingers, the moon and the stars, which Thou hast ordained."

And in Isaiah 64:8 we read, "But now, O Lord, Thou art our Father, we are the clay, and Thou our potter; And all of us are the work of Thy hand."

God has made us into the exact unique mold of the perfect plan and person He wants us to be. If God is the potter and we are the clay, then we truly are a masterpiece, each one of us, fashioned by the work of the Master's hand!

This Next Week:

We all may feel imperfect at times, but remember that God did create us and we are all the work of His hand. Encourage each other this week, maybe it's compliments, or simple words of affirmation, but really love your partner for the unique individual they are. And tell them so!

Notes, special thoughts, and prayers for my baby.

_____
_____
_____
_____
_____
_____
_____
_____
_____
_____
_____
_____
_____
_____
_____
_____
_____
_____
_____
_____
_____
_____
_____

Week 19

So your baby is weighing in at approximately half a pound this week, and give or take about six inches long. Your baby also now has a protective layer called the vernix, covering all of his skin from the amniotic fluid. It's a greasy white substance, which doesn't sound very cute, but it will shed before delivery, unless your baby decides to show up early. But it's a good covering! It helps baby's skin to not get all wrinkled, think overly wrinkled bathtub toes!

This "covering of protection" for baby is a reminder of God's constant covering of protection in our lives. We live in a fallen world—full of sickness, despair, grieving, and sin and sometimes we do not understand the workings and will of God in our lives. But we do know, that through all things, God's protection for us comes in many forms. Sometimes it is an end to a despair that we could not see ahead, it may be in a form of peace and comforting in a desperate situation. God is our provider and protector in all things and with new life in Him, His love for us will always be our protection. We can trust in this!

What do the Scriptures say?

2 Thessalonians 3:3 says, "But the Lord is faithful; He will strengthen you and protect you from the evil one."

Deuteronomy 31:6 says, "Be strong and courageous, do not be afraid or tremble at them, for the Lord your God is the One who goes with you."

This Next Week:

Study your Bible and read the many Scriptures of promises the Lord gives us about His love and protection over us. Start with Psalm 5, a prayer of protection from the wicked, and Psalm 6, a prayer for mercy in times of trouble. His Word promises this to us over and over. Pray and thank Him for protection over yourselves, your household, and your little baby, always!

Notes, special thoughts, and prayers for my baby.

_____
_____
_____
_____
_____
_____
_____
_____
_____
_____
_____
_____
_____
_____
_____
_____
_____
_____
_____
_____
_____

Week 20

Welcome to the halfway mark! Week 20 of 40. Can you believe it's already half over? If this first half has gone really fast for you, make sure to take in every moment of the last half. It's a very special time! If you are already feeling like you are ready to speed things up, well, you're halfway there, girl! It will be over before you know it!

This is also about the time when you get to possibly find out the gender of your baby. Boy or girl? Can you wait to find out? Or are you anxious with anticipation to find out already so you can pick out a name and buy all your nursery items and start nesting? Whatever you decided, it will be the right choice for you and your partner!

I'm sure by now you may have a list going of all of your favorite names. My husband and I had an ongoing list, and we pared down as time went on. Since we didn't find out the gender until delivery, we narrowed it down, and wanted to decide for sure when we actually saw and met our baby. We wanted to be thoughtful about it.

Meanings of names were important to us as well. It was the whole package, I guess you could say. I wanted to have a good strong name, a good strong meaning, and have the name suit the little face I would set my eyes on. We prayed that we could agree on all of these things and that God would help us settle on a name that would suit the little person He was creating for us!

What do the Scriptures say?

Names in the Bible tend to hold a lot of meaning and the Lord even changed some people's name after a life-altering event, to give their name a greater, stronger meaning.

In Proverbs 22:1 it says, "A good name is to be more desired than great riches, favor is better than silver and gold."

This Next Week:

I do think that it is a good idea to pray with your partner about a good name for your child. Yes, choose names you are both happy with, but also seek out their meanings and origin. Make it a thoughtful choice and pray on your choices. It's a name that will stay with them through their entire lives and possibly define certain things about them. Remember also, they are the ones who have to live with it, so be kind.

Notes, special thoughts, and prayers for my baby.

_____
_____
_____
_____
_____
_____
_____
_____
_____
_____
_____
_____
_____
_____
_____
_____
_____
_____
_____
_____
_____
_____
_____

Week 21

*B*aby is about the size of a banana this week, its arms and legs are finally in proportion and cartilage through the body is turning into bone, which is helping baby to be so much more coordinated in its movements. Hopefully you may have been feeling this by now too!

Your baby is still practicing swallowing as well, and is taking in the amniotic fluids your body is producing each day. Which also means it's tasting different types of food you are eating! Baby is developing a taste for what you eat, so keep it healthy and keep those good foods coming on your daily menu!

We thrive on the good foods we eat, and God has given them to us to enjoy since the beginning of creation when He created the earth and all things upon it.

What do the Scriptures say?

In Genesis 1:29–30 it says, "Then God said, Behold, I have given you every plant yielding seed that is on the surface of all the earth, and every tree which has fruit yielding seed; it shall be food for you; and to every beast of the earth and to every bird of the sky and to everything that moves on the earth which has life, I have given every green plant for food; and it was so."

God has provided all our needs since the beginning of time so we may thrive and be healthy and benefit from all these provisions.

This Next Week:

As I know you have already been doing, continue to make good choices in your eating habits for the benefit of you and your partner's health now, and to live a long healthy life, but to also continue to enrich your tiny baby with the good nutrients God has given us to grow and thrive. Make these good choices now and continue to implement them after your baby is born to keep up the good eating habits you have started! And as with every meal, remember to always take the time to pray and thank the Lord for all He provides for you!

Notes, special thoughts, and
prayers for my baby.

_____
_____
_____
_____
_____
_____
_____
_____
_____
_____
_____
_____
_____
_____
_____
_____
_____
_____
_____
_____
_____
_____
_____
_____
_____
_____
_____
_____
_____
_____

Week 22

Your little one has tipped the scale this week at approximately one whole pound! Whoa, baby! When you start weighing in pounds, you know there's some serious growing happening! Your baby is continuing to develop its senses and is growing continually more sensitive to its surroundings of touch, sight, taste, and sound. Although baby still has its eyes closed, you can try that trick of shining a flashlight around your belly to see if you can get a reaction and some movement happening.

I have always loved the idea that my son is the only person who will ever know what my heart sounds like from the inside, or the loud sound of my blood circulating through my body. And baby is still hearing all the sounds from the outside as well. Not just your voice, but all the background noise as well.

We have read about our sense of hearing and how important it is to make sure that we are listening and taking in good things, especially because we want our baby to hear only good things! As we continue to speak words of life and truth to our baby, remember to intentionally speak the Word of God to your baby even now. Let your little one hear the gospel on a daily basis!

What do the Scriptures say?

"So faith comes from hearing, and hearing by the word of Christ." (Rom. 10:17)

"He who has ears to hear, let him hear." (Matt. 11:15)

"And the seed in the good soil, these are the ones who have heard the word in an honest and good heart, and hold it fast, and bear fruit with perseverance." (Luke 8:15)

This Next Week:

We are taught and reminded throughout the Bible to listen and hear. Focus in on your baby's hearing and do your devotions out loud, read the Word of God out loud and speak to your baby about God's promises. Why wait until we think they are old enough to understand? The Word of God is life and should be spoken to all who can hear it.

*Notes, special thoughts, and
prayers for my baby.*

_____

_____

_____

_____

_____

_____

_____

_____

_____

_____

_____

_____

_____

_____

_____

_____

_____

_____

_____

_____

_____

_____

_____

_____

_____

_____

_____

CHAPTER 6

The Sixth Month

Weeks 23-27

These next few weeks mark the last phase of your second trimester, and not only does that make you close to the "two-thirds of the way done" mark, it's also that much closer to seeing, touching, smelling, and holding your perfect little bundle of joy!

By now you most likely have had your most intensive ultrasound (if you are opting for doing them) where they do a thorough check of all of your baby's parts and make sure that everything is developing as it should. It can be a lengthy appointment, but it's quite fun to see all the different angles and different vantage points of your little one squirming and wiggling up a storm!

I will share with you that I was scared at this appointment. I let fear and doubt and worry enter my mind, and I cried most of the ride to the appointment. I was terrified of finding something abnormal in the scans and instead of praying for comfort and peace and keeping my trust in the Lord, I let the natural feelings of negativity creep in and worry me. I really think evil loves these moments. It sees us having a weak moment and seizes the opportunity to make it even worse.

My husband was always my biggest encourager during these times and helped to reassure me and calm my nerves and pray when I sometimes couldn't find the words myself. Husbands, remember to be the rock for your wife. She needs you there, whether she asks you or not!

I would encourage you during these appointments, whether you have had many at this point, you still need to go, or maybe you have chosen to go more natural, but to pray before you leave your house and ask God to go before you, and then go with you. We know He is our protector and shield and no matter what the outcomes, He has already made a way that we cannot yet see.

Trust Him that He has the best laid plans for you and your family and baby. He truly does. I am often reminded of that very well-known poem "Footprints," as I think of many instances in my life where I needed the Lord to carry me:

One night I dreamed a dream.
I was walking along the beach with my Lord.
Across the dark sky flashed scenes from my life.
For each scene, I noticed two sets of footprints in the sand,
one belonging to me and one to my Lord.

After the last scene of my life flashed before me,
I looked back at the footprints in the sand.
I noticed that at many times along the path of my life,
especially at the very lowest and saddest times,
there was only one set of footprints.

This really troubled me, so I asked the Lord about it.
"Lord, you said once I decided to follow You,
You'd walk with me all the way.
But I noticed that during the saddest and
most troublesome times of my life,
there was only one set of footprints.
I don't understand why, when I needed You the most,
You would leave me."

He whispered, "My precious child, I love
you and will never leave you,

86

never, ever, during your trials and testings.
When you saw only one set of footprints,
It was then that I carried you."

Week 23

Your baby is still growing, fast as ever and since skin grows a little faster than the developing fat, baby's skin is still a bit saggy and still transparent. Don't worry though, by the time baby arrives, it will have beautiful chubby little limbs so adorable you will not be able to help yourself from kissing each little roll and fold!

It's interesting to know that since the skin is still transparent, you can still see the organs and bones that are growing! The skin has a bit of a red hue to it because of the continuing developing blood veins and arteries underneath.

It is truly amazing what we know about medicine in today's world. We can literally pinpoint the growth of our babies in the womb on a daily basis to know exactly when certain development happens and see pictures and video of what it looks like inside of us.

The Bible speaks of our anatomy and how we were fitted together, ultimately to be pieced together for the building up of itself in love. Isn't that beautiful?

What do the Scriptures say?

In Ephesians chapter 4, the entire chapter speaks of the unity of the Spirit. Read the entire chapter through, but pay close attention to verses 15 and 16. "But speaking the truth in love, we are to grow up in all aspects into Him, who is the head, even Christ, from whom the whole body, being fitted and held together by that which every joint supplies, according to the proper working of each individual part, causes the growth of the body for the building up of itself in love."

This Next Week:

Remember in prayer this week to be thankful for not only the building up of our bodies, but also the significance of the building up of the body of Christ from this chapter you have read through in Ephesians. Just as you are to have grown up in all aspects into Him, so should you teach and train your children to do so. Pray that you and your partner will be walking in a manner worthy of the calling with which you have been called, with humility and gentleness and patience, as the Word of the Lord says!

Notes, special thoughts, and prayers for my baby.

Week 24

*Y*our tiny baby continues to grow, with its face almost fully formed, more fat continuing to accumulate, and did you know that your baby's hair color is not a color yet? So far the hair color on its head is actually snow white! This is because there is no pigment there yet, but it will come.

You may have a good idea of what color that hair will end up being. If you and your partner are both dark featured, there's a good chance that your baby will be as well, but that's the fun part—you won't really know until you see him or her!

There are so many things about your child that you get to learn that you won't know until you meet them. What an exciting thought. What will they look like is the obvious question, but what about their personality, likes and dislikes? God knows all of this already! As we read before in Jeremiah 1:5 where it says, "Before I formed you in the womb I knew you, and before you were born I consecrated you; I appointed you a prophet to the nations."

Your little one has a plan and a purpose and God knows exactly who they will be and what that purpose will be. Aren't you proud already? You should be!

What do the Scriptures say?

In Jeremiah 29:11 we read, "For I know the plans I have for you, declares the Lord, plans for welfare and not for calamity to give you a future and a hope."

God has the best plans already laid out for our children, and there's no better plan than His. What a huge relief to know we can trust in this promise!

This Next Week:

It's never too early to pray for our children's futures. Keep this in mind this week. Ask God to take control of this little life and their future. For we know that His plans for this child are great, and filled with hope. What more could we possibly want for our children!

Notes, special thoughts, and prayers for my baby.

Week 25

*L*eaps and bounds of growth are still happening with baby at about nine inches in length and around one and a half pounds. The capillaries are forming and filling with blood, and air sacs lined with capillaries will develop in the lungs. Eventually this will finish forming the lungs so your baby will be ready to take that first breath of air. The nostrils are also beginning to open up this week, which will help it to practice more breathing for the big day.

So many intricate developments continue to unfold in your womb and they are all so precise and perfect, they could only be made by our Creator! We can thank God for this divine work and for the health of our bodies that carry this baby, and the health of the baby He is creating. God promises us divine health in the Bible when we make Him our dwelling place—a 24/7 relationship with Him.

What do the Scriptures say?

In Psalm 91:9–10 it says, "Because you have made the Lord, who is my refuge, even the Most High, your dwelling place, no evil shall befall you, nor shall any plague come near your dwelling."

God is telling us simply that if we dwell with Him, He will dwell with us, protecting your home from evil and blessing everyone in the home. We can declare these promises and believe them for our families.

This Next Week:

Read this passage of Scripture over and over until it becomes a daily part of your prayer life. Make God your dwelling place, and ask for divine health for yourself and your family.

Notes, special thoughts, and prayers for my baby.

_____

_____

_____

_____

_____

_____

_____

_____

_____

_____

_____

_____

_____

_____

_____

_____

_____

_____

_____

_____

_____

_____

_____

_____

_____

Week 26

O kay, so your baby is about two pounds now! Boy, is that little one growing quickly! And so exciting this week, the eyelids are slowly beginning to open. Your baby can't see much as it's pretty dark in that small, confined space, but with its already heightened sense of light, you might notice that your baby moves around a bit more when it does see a bright light, or hears a loud noise. It may be opening its eyes to see if it can see what is going on outside in that great big world!

It's a strange thing to think that your child has so much to learn, everything in fact! It will all be new for your little one and you will be the person they will rely on for answers, keeping them safe, anticipating their needs, and loving them so much.

God loves us so much and knows all our needs before we even know we need anything! Just like a parent, He watches over us, knows our hearts and hears our prayers, and He answers us, in just the right time.

What do the Scriptures say?

In Isaiah 65:23–24 is says, "They shall not labor in vain, nor bring forth children for trouble; for they shall be the descendants of the blessed of the Lord, and their offspring with them. It shall come to pass that before they call, I will answer; and while they are still speaking, I will hear."

God knows what we need before we do. If we, as earthly parents, love our children enough to meet all of their needs before they ask us, can you imagine how much more God can provide for us? We are so blessed to be loved by our heavenly Father.

This Next Week:

Pray for God's divine covering for yourself and your child, and that you will not need to face anything in life without the grace and care already supplied ahead of time, and right when we need it. Thank Him for His constant blessings and anticipating our every need before we even ask!

Notes, special thoughts, and prayers for my baby.

Week 27

*Y*our baby is now officially being measured from head to toe from now on! No more crown to rump for this little one. At about fifteen inches, baby is just over a foot tall. Not so little anymore! How exciting to know that this little baby is continually growing in leaps and bounds and it's still full steam ahead.

Everything about your baby's growth is exciting and miraculous and should be celebrated. We are all created for God's glory, and we should constantly be in worshipful awe as to what is really unfolding!

What do the Scriptures say?

In Isaiah 43:5–7 we read, "Fear not, for I am with you; I will bring your descendants from the east, and gather you from the west; I will say to the north, "give them up!" and to the south "Do not keep them back!" Bring My sons from afar, and My daughters from the ends of the earth—everyone who is called by My name, whom I have created for My glory; I have formed him, yes, I have made him."

God refers to our children as His sons and daughters. He is telling us that "because they belong to you, they belong to Me."

This Next Week:

Give God all the glory and thanks for the life He has created inside of you, for we are all His children and are all created to glorify Him.

Notes, special thoughts, and prayers for my baby.

_____
_____
_____
_____
_____
_____
_____
_____
_____
_____
_____
_____
_____
_____
_____
_____
_____
_____
_____
_____
_____
_____
_____

CHAPTER 7

The Seventh Month

Weeks 28–31

You have made it! Welcome to your third and final trimester! You are now only three short months away from holding your beautiful baby and falling madly in love. These next three months will slow you down a bit, make you feel like you are carrying a heavier load than you thought you could carry, and the excitement and probably anxious feelings of labor and delivery will surely follow as well.

Really enjoy these last three months. Sleep as much as you possibly can, get everything ready for baby's arrival, have someone help you clean your house, and if you have the energy, I would even suggest doing some freezer cooking. You may have lots of family and friends to come over and help you when your little one comes home, but there are many days between those visits when you still need to eat and the last thing you want to do is cook a big meal. I spent a couple of weeks making preportioned meals for my husband and I, and let me tell you, it saved me! We still had good nutritious food to eat without having to think about takeout or reaching for the bad stuff!

You will never really know exactly how things will work at home until baby actually comes home and you get yourself into a routine that works for you all, but getting organized while you can still get around and have some energy left in you is a good idea. Don't wait too long either. With each passing week, you will start to drag a bit more, and you really don't want to overexert yourself and do too much at the end. Let others help you when they offer. They know how it feels to be in your shoes, and they are just as excited to help you in any way possible!

Take that well deserved nap from now on!

Week 28

*Y*our baby has begun to blink those precious little eyelids this week, along with what they have been practicing for some time now—coughing, sucking practice breaths, and even hiccupping! The lungs are almost fully mature now as well. Your baby still has so much more growing to do, but it's nice to know that some of those basic needs to get them into this world are ready to go when it's time!

As time will most likely go quite quickly for you from here on out, have you and your partner really talked about, or grasped the idea that in only a few short weeks you are going to be parents? You are already responsible and accountable to each other, but you will now be completely responsible for a new little life, completely reliant on you both. And not just for the baby stages, but their entire life. It's a real major life change when our little ones are born.

I already consider you parents at this stage in fact. You are already taking care of that little one each day and bonding with them even in the womb. They know you are there just as much as you know they are. The moment they enter the world is the moment you become Mom and Dad to this wee one. It's a name that only that little baby will call you, and it's an honor and an incredible feeling.

One thing that struck me when I had my son was that I finally understood how my own parents must have felt when I was born. I then realized what it meant to love someone so completely unconditionally, and that with just one look at them, you would give your life to save theirs without hesitation. I then appreciated my own parents in a new light. I thought about how much they have loved me throughout my life. It was overwhelming!

What do the Scriptures say?

Through my life I always loved my parents, but I did not always honor them and respect them as the Bible instructs us to. I can remember very specific times of rebellion, and I know I've hurt them and worried them. Looking back, I can't imagine how they would have felt. I know now how I would feel if my son would do the same!

We all know the verse in Exodus 20:12 that tell us, "Honor your Father and Mother, that your days may be prolonged in the land which the Lord your God gives you." The Lord has instructed us to honor our parents. Do we? Even though we are older now and about to become parents ourselves, it's still important. As we age our relationships with our families change, but the respect and honor we should show our parents should not. This should also be something that you talk about in your home with your child as they grow and model this behavior in front of them to your own parents—their grandparents. Nothing but respect should be shown and taught.

This Next Week:

Some of us have wonderful family relationships and others do not. But it's not too late to mend or change that. We are to forgive as Christ forgives us. Whatever your relationship with your own parents, make an effort to acknowledge them as the people you honor and respect and tell them so. Very soon you will be in their shoes and will hope for and expect the same from your own child. It's a little humbling to think on, but very rewarding. Your child will respect you when they see you model it firsthand!

Notes, special thoughts, and
prayers for my baby.

_____

_____

_____

_____

_____

_____

_____

_____

_____

_____

_____

_____

_____

_____

_____

_____

_____

_____

_____

_____

_____

_____

_____

Week 29

*Y*our baby is around three pounds and in the next eleven weeks he or she will at least double in weight by the time they make their exit. That's a lot of weight in a short time, but all good and ultra-adorable baby fat that will make their already cute little faces and bodies so squishy perfect you won't be able to handle the cuteness!

As parents we automatically think our child is perfect and the cutest and the smartest. It's totally normal and we all do it. I think it's okay to think that way because we are just so proud of our little ones and constantly in awe of how quickly they grow and learn, and because they are a part of us we can't help but shine when they do even the smallest things.

I do, however, think that there is that fine line in parenting where we all question our own selves when it comes to spoiling a child, or how we discipline them. We are after all, their parents, not their friends. Have you already spoken with your partner about your thoughts on discipline? Now would be the time. A tiny baby does not need discipline in the early stages, but even so, they are smart from day one and it helps to be consistent with routines and the way they are cared for. You really want to make sure you both have an idea of what the other expects and really be honest with each other now. Be open to each other's suggestions. It's possibly the first time for both of you. Nobody is right or wrong, and you will most definitely make mistakes. Make them together, without blame. And maybe laugh along the way about it too! You will try to be perfect, but you can't be and you won't be.

What do the Scriptures say?

When it comes to the raising of a child, you both need to pray about this, seek the Lord and the Word and communicate with each other. However you decide to train, teach, and discipline your child will be your chosen way. Stick with it and be consistent, and don't let too many people interfere. You will ultimately know what is best for them. And even more than that, remember that God is still the one who has their best plan laid out for them. Respect that and remind yourself of the verse in Proverbs 22:6 "Train up a child in the way he should go, even when he is old he will not depart from it."

This Next Week:

The training of our children is a massive responsibility and should not be taken lightly. Read books on parenting, seek advice from those closest to you, talk with each other about how you think you should approach things—always making sure it's a team effort! And most importantly, remember to include God as the first person you seek help from and ask for direction from. He will guide you and honor your faithfulness as parents!

Notes, special thoughts, and prayers for my baby.

_____
_____
_____
_____
_____
_____
_____
_____
_____
_____
_____
_____
_____
_____
_____
_____
_____
_____
_____
_____
_____
_____
_____
_____

Week 30

As your baby is still growing, his or her brain is also getting bigger and taking on those grooves and indentations. The wrinkles allow for expansion in the future as your baby grows into a responsive infant, to a toddler, and beyond.

It's amazing how fast our littles ones learn. They learn immediately that if they cry, someone will come and help them with whatever it is they need. Babies are incredibly intelligent and it won't take long for them to outsmart you, trust me!

These family relationships will begin immediately when you come home with your baby. Both Mom and Dad provide special roles and fulfill certain needs for baby and they will come to learn that. In everything, make sure that your caring for the baby, your discipline, and teaching are consistent with each other and in line with what the Bible teaches us.

Because our babies do learn so fast, even as infants, remember to make sure that your home is filled with love, in the way you speak, the things you say to each other and to the baby, and that what you listen to is pure and clean. Baby is absorbing everything, just as it was when it was in the womb.

What do the Scriptures say?

Another reminder of training and bringing our children up the way God asks of us is in Ephesians 6:12 where is says, "And fathers, do not provoke your children to anger, but bring them up in the discipline and instructions of the Lord."

It refers to fathers, but please make this both of your responsibility, all the time. The Bible regards our husbands and fathers as the head of our homes, and ultimately that should be respected, but wives and mothers are to honor these instructions the same.

This Next Week:

Take special time to pray for one another openly. That your partner will be strong and capable and seek the Lord for direction and that you, as their partner, will be a steadfast prayer warrior for them, a shoulder to lean on, and the helpmate you were designed to be for them. Your relationship is still a priority to your family's health and well-being. Take time together to be united and stay strong in the Lord, in a God-centered marriage!

Notes, special thoughts, and prayers for my baby.

_____

_____

_____

_____

_____

_____

_____

_____

_____

_____

_____

_____

_____

_____

_____

_____

_____

_____

_____

_____

_____

_____

_____

_____

_____

_____

_____

_____

Week 31

*Y*ou may notice that you have longer stretches of "quiet time" with baby as they now sleep longer in their REM sleep! Then when they do wake up, they may be much more alert, and for longer, with some pretty defined moving. They may even have a pretty regular sleep schedule already if you have a normal routine that you stick to as well!

As we have looked at parenting and training our children as we are instructed to these past few weeks, I look back and remember one constant thought when I was carrying my son. I knew that with God's help and the support of my husband and our families, we were going to be all right, as long as our house was a household of faith.

Yes, I was aware that I was going to make mistakes and was not going to be a perfect parent, but I did know that I was capable of doing my best and that as long as I trusted in the Lord and did right by His Word and His teachings, all the things I had learned and held dear throughout my life, all His promises to us, His never ending love and grace He gives us just when we need it, I knew that despite my overwhelming fear at times about how I was going to be as a mother to my child, I knew I was not alone.

What do the Scriptures say?

We have all heard this verse and seen it on signs or posters in churches or plaques, but how often have you really meant it and prayed for this sincerely? In Joshua 24:15 we read, "And if it is disagreeable in your sight to serve the Lord, choose for yourself today whom you will serve; whether the gods which your fathers served which were beyond the River, or the gods of the Amorites in whose land you are living; *but as for me and my house, we will serve the Lord.*"

As for me and my house, we will serve the Lord. This is a statement and a declaration I make for my home every day. We *will* and we do serve the Lord. In all ways. We want our house to be a home that our son grows up in and knows the Lord. It is our responsibility to teach him, and for him to hear about the Lord first, from us.

This Next Week:

Make your home a home that is serving the Lord if you haven't already. Invite the Lord to live in your home and dwell with you and within you. Part of nesting can be your spiritual nesting as well. Your child will thrive in a home that loves the Lord and they will learn from this example and create a home of their own the same way one day. Every day remind yourself, believe it, and act upon this verse.

Notes, special thoughts, and prayers for my baby.

CHAPTER 8

The Eighth Month

Weeks 32–35

The eighth month! Wow! With every month, week, and day that passes, I can only imagine the excitement you are feeling. I truly hope that you are feeling well and enjoying this special time. I've said it many times, but it goes so fast and it is such a beautiful experience. Take in every moment. I know during these last weeks it might feel long and hard and you will surely want to be done so you can finally hold your beautiful reward at the end of it, but remember to stop and enjoy the peaceful moments.

This physical connection with your baby is truly the most amazing feeling a person can have, I believe. The fact that God is weaving together new life inside your body is miraculous.

Life is a gift from God and He speaks of the promise of life for us in Deuteronomy 30:19–20 where it says, "I call heaven and earth to witness against you today, that I have set before you life and death, the blessing and the curse. So choose life in order that you may live, you and your descendants, by loving the Lord your God, by obeying His voice, and by holding fast to Him; for this is your life and the length of your days, that you may live in the land which the Lord swore to your fathers, to Abraham, Isaac, and Jacob, to give them."

This passage can be read as a promise of a long wonderful life for you and your family. If you choose life in your lives and your home, you will be blessed and this will also be passed to your children as well.

Speak life and live life in all you do as a family and in your home, and live the promises God has for you!

Week 32

*A*s your baby still continues to pack on a few more pounds before the big day, his or her skin is no longer see-through. Baby finally has enough "meat" on it, so its skin is now opaque, just like yours! Oh my, just wait until you can feel that perfect baby skin for the first time. It is the softest, most beautiful skin.

Speaking of beautiful, *you* are beautiful. You are a beautiful woman, carrying a beautiful gift inside of you. I really hope you hold on to that and I hope your partner reminds you often!

One beautiful woman in my life was my grandma. I had a special relationship with her and she was one of my closest confidants. She was a woman of great worth and character and was a role model for me, for who I wanted to be when I grew up, and became a wife and mother. I feel I may never live up to her grace, but I at least have a bar set very high for me to try to achieve some level of the God-fearing woman she was. She was such a blessing to our family.

What do the Scriptures say?

In saying that, I would like you to read through Proverbs 31:10–31. This passage of Scripture should be a challenge for you today and through your life. It surely has been and still is for me. I desire to be a God-fearing wife and mother who works hard for her family.

Verses 28–31 specifically read, "Her children rise up and bless her; her husband also, and he praises her saying; 'Many daughters have done nobly, but you excel them all.' Charm is deceitful and beauty is vain, but a woman who fears the Lord, she shall be praised. Give her the product of her hands, And let her works praise her in the gates."

This Next Week:

Challenge yourself, as a wife and a mother, to this description of a worthy woman, who we should all strive to be. I believe it may take our entire lives to truly be this, as it's a lifelong journey, but evaluate your life and how you can improve and be the best woman you can be. For yourself and your family!

*Notes, special thoughts, and
prayers for my baby.*

Week 33

aby is probably gaining about a half a pound a week at this point and you are definitely going to notice that and fast! He or she is really running out of room in there and you may notice that baby is still moving but because of the limited space, the jabs and kicks are pretty hard and most likely quite uncomfortable.

Antibodies are being passed from you to baby as well. It is developing its own immune system and that's really great, because we all know a good immune system sure does come in handy out here in the outside world!

We live in a world full of sickness, and yes, we do catch flus and colds, but as we spoke of earlier, you can still pray for a healthy pregnancy and safety for your baby after it is born. God died for us and by His stripes we are healed. It's important to believe these things and hold on to His promises.

What do the Scriptures say?

We can read more verses that speak of healing and good health that is promised to us.

> 3 John 1:2 says, "Beloved, I pray that in all respects you may prosper and be in good health, just as your soul prospers." (3 John 1:2)

> "Is anyone among you sick? Let him call for the elders of the church, and let them pray over him, anointing him with oil in the name of the Lord; and the prayer offered in faith will restore the one who is sick, and the Lord will raise him up, and if he has committed sins, they will be forgiven him." (James 5:14–15)

"And He Himself bore our sins in His body on the cross, that we might die to sin and live to righteousness." (1 Peter 2:24)

This Next Week:

Continue to pray for health and well-being so that you can enjoy these last weeks and your body will remain strong and healthy for baby as well.

Notes, special thoughts, and prayers for my baby.

_____
_____
_____
_____
_____
_____
_____
_____
_____
_____
_____
_____
_____
_____
_____
_____
_____
_____
_____
_____
_____
_____
_____
_____
_____
_____

Week 34

A t approximately five pounds and maybe around twenty inches or so, your baby is tipping the scales and there are no signs of stopping just yet! If you know that you are having a boy, then you may know that his testicles are making their way down from his abdomen to their final destination as well. And in other developing news, the tiny little fingernails on your baby's fingers have about reached the tips of its fingers! Oh, that tiny little hand, so perfectly formed. Just wait until you have them grab your finger for the first time. It happens so naturally, and it will make you swoon. Like, really swoon.

Our children are such a blessing to us and bring us such joy. God our Father loves our children even more than we ourselves do, which is so hard to imagine, but He does.

What do the Scriptures say?

In Matthew 19:13–15, Jesus blessed the little children. "Then some children were brought to Him so that He might lay His hands on them and pray; and the disciples rebuked them. But Jesus said, 'Let the children alone, and do not hinder them from coming to Me; for the kingdom of heaven belongs to such as these.' And after laying His hands on them, He departed from there."

This Scripture reminds me of the old simple song we all know, "Jesus loves me this I know." We all sang it as children in Sunday school, and we remember seeing images of the children sitting around Jesus as He spoke to them and blessed them. Jesus does love our children more than we ever could and we can take so much comfort in knowing that He cares for them. When we can't be beside them, we can always know that the Lord is.

This Next Week:

Thank God for loving your baby. He created this little being and entrusted it to you, that you will raise it in the ways of the Lord. He loves your little one as much as He loves you, and died for your child on the cross as well.

Notes, special thoughts, and prayers for my baby.

_____
_____
_____
_____
_____
_____
_____
_____
_____
_____
_____
_____
_____
_____
_____
_____
_____
_____
_____
_____
_____
_____
_____

Week 35

*Y*our baby's brain cells are still hard at work, making the head a little larger all the time, but don't worry, the head is still soft, which will make the trip through the birth canal very manageable!

You may have noticed that your baby has already positioned its head down toward your pelvis and is slowly but surely getting ready to make that final journey out into the world. Your doctor will keep an eye on this to make sure your baby's head stays in that position for the final drop, but some little ones do decide to make a few last-minute adjustments and do flip breach position at the last minute. Your doctor will know exactly what to do!

Speaking of your baby moving inside of you, a feeling you are well used to by now (and one you may miss a little once they come out!), I was always reminded of the story of Mary and Elizabeth in the book of Luke.

What do the Scriptures say?

In Luke 1:39–45 the chapter reads, "Now at this time Mary arose and went with haste to the hill country, to a city of Judah, and entered the house of Zacharias and greeted Elizabeth. And it came about that when Elizabeth heard Mary's greeting, the baby leaped in her womb; and Elizabeth was filled with the Holy Spirit. And she cried out with a loud voice, and said, 'Blessed among women are you, and blessed is the fruit of your womb! And how has it happened to me that the mother of my Lord should come to me? For behold, when the sound of your greeting reached my ears, the baby leaped in my womb for joy. And blessed is she who believed that there would be a fulfillment of what had been spoken to her by the Lord.'"

Although none of us could ever imagine what it would have been like for Elizabeth to have experienced this amazing meeting, or especially Mary, the mother of Jesus to have carried her own Lord and

Savior in her womb, we as expectant mothers are somehow moved by this story in a special way that only a mother carrying a child can understand.

This Next Week:

Thank God for sending His Son, Jesus, into this world as a baby. As it says in Luke 2:12 "And this will be a sign for you; you will find a baby wrapped in cloths, and lying in a manger." He humbled Himself for me, for you, and our children, so we could find salvation through Him. He paid the highest price for us, which was to die and take our sins upon Himself, so we could be saved and forgiven, through the shedding of His blood.

Notes, special thoughts, and prayers for my baby.

CHAPTER 9

The Ninth Month

Weeks 36-40

I feel like there should be a drumroll here, but ta-da! You made it to your ninth month! Congratulations, you have come a long way, lady!

Doctor's visits will be weekly now, unless your doctor has specified more, and there will be so many things you will want to get finished up and ready before baby gets here in a few short weeks.

I am one of those super organized people that makes lists, and actually gets them done and I don't like to procrastinate, so at this point, for me, I was pretty much ready. The nursery was fully stocked and decorated, I was coming to the end of my work time to take my leave and that was all ready to let go as well. The things I did for myself in the last two weeks was I got my hair and nails done so I would feel well groomed once baby arrived. My husband and I went on dinner dates and had a lot of fun as a couple. We knew our time of just being "us two" was close to over, and I didn't take that for granted.

I really encourage you do something like that. Go out with your friends, maybe go away for a night or two with your husband and stay in a fancy hotel. It's the last vacation for a while on your own; go for it! Eat out a few more times than normal in nice restaurants, read a few books, take more naps . . .

Week 36

Your baby is around six pounds and somewhere around twenty inches or so and most of the systems are all ready to go for this little one, but the digestive system, although formed, hasn't really gotten a workout yet. As soon as baby is out and you nurse for the first time, the digestive system will kick into full gear and the system will be jump started.

Whether you read a lot of books or watched videos about childbirth, or you attended a birthing class, I'm sure you understand what is going to happen very soon. It's a little unnerving right? Toward the end of my pregnancy, I found a show that would come on television at 5:00 a.m. That's right, folks, 5:00 a.m. What was I thinking? Anyway, the show was about real-life mothers giving birth in hospitals. I would somehow wake up every morning right at 5:00 a.m. and freak myself out. My husband would wake up to go to work and just shake his head. I would be sitting there eating a snack and balling my eyes out at the perfect little newborns and the happy families welcoming them. I was pretty emotional at that point. I'll just leave it at that.

Even though people can coach you over and over and in different ways about what is to come, you really won't get it until you get to that point. So I'm going to be one of those people now who says something like "don't worry about it! You'll be fine!" and you will roll your eyes, but honestly, you will be fine. It just all somehow works out and you just know what to do, and your doctor knows what to do.

What do the Scriptures say?

Have you ever heard people say that you "somehow forget how bad childbirth was and just keep wanting to have another child?" or something similar? Did you know that there's a verse in the Bible that says this, and Jesus Himself said it. In John 16:21–22, Jesus says, "Whenever a woman is in travail she has sorrow, because her hour has come; but when she gives birth to the child, she remembers the anguish no more, for joy that a child has been born into the world.

Therefore you too now have sorrow; but I will see you again and your heart will rejoice, and no one will take your joy away from you."

This verse was a comfort to me, long after I had my son, just in knowing that even in those times which may not seem important to anyone but us, God has thought them through and knows the pain a woman will go through, but will let her forget so she can bear to do it again. It's really a wonderful blessing and so amazing . . . God really is in the details.

This Next Week:

As anxious as you may be feeling, trust in God, pray together for His comfort and peace as you go through this next week. Thank Him now for what is going to happen as He already knows the time your baby will arrive and has it all worked out for you. It's nice to know the doctor is going to be there waiting for you, but remember that God is going to be in the room with you as well. Praise Him for that!

Notes, special thoughts, and prayers for my baby.

Week 37

*D*id you know that if your baby would be born today, you would actually be considered full term? Baby is not at all finished growing, but he or she would be very ready for the outside world and very strong and developed.

God's timing is perfect. Right from the beginning of your pregnancy, He knew exactly when your baby would be born. The day, the hour, the minute. There is a time appointed for your little one and that time is God's time, which is the perfect time. It's so hard for us to wait at times though, isn't it?

What do the Scriptures say?

In Ecclesiastes 3:1–9, I would encourage you to read the entire passage, but let's focus on verses 1–2. "There is an appointed time for everything. And there is a time for every event under heaven. A time to give birth, and a time to die."

Patience really is a virtue and this may be your most virtuous time of your life as you wait out the next while for baby's arrival. Trust in the Lord that He has already gone before you to let your child enter this world at just the right time—His time!

This Next Week:

Pray for patience and peace as you wait and continue to get ready for your little one's arrival. Rest in knowing that God has your life and your baby's life safely in His plans. You can rejoice in knowing that you are not alone and so very loved and thought of!

Notes, special thoughts, and prayers for my baby.

Week 38

*I*f your baby is still inside your tummy, he or she is most likely still growing. Could be up to seven pounds by now. Everyone is different though, and don't worry much about that. Whether your baby is a little smaller or a little bigger doesn't matter as long as they are happy and healthy. Everyone guessed I would have a huge baby, but my son was six pounds thirteen ounces and nineteen inches long. So not that big at all. I know of very petite girls with ten-pound babies and they did just fine as well. So will you!

Things can move quickly these last two weeks, or more or less depending on your situation. For me, I had a quick spike in blood pressure in my thirty-eighth week and my doctor kept a very close eye on it daily and we decided to induce my labor at thirty-nine weeks.

I was very scared and troubled at the time, and looking back, I know it's because it was a first-time experience for both my husband and I, and we trusted our doctor and I have no regrets that it happened that way. I think we often get a funny idea in our head about how it should be. We see in movies that the woman wakes up at 2:00 a.m. and her water breaks and they rush to the hospital and she has the baby. Well, that's not quite how it happens in real life! Did you know that most women don't actually even have their water break until they are at the hospital in labor?

Looking back, however, although I was nervous at times, one thing remained—I had a spirit of thankfulness that I will always remember. I felt so very thankful for what the Lord was about to give me. I felt like the richest, luckiest girl in the world.

What do the Scriptures say?

> "Always giving thanks for all things in the name of our Lord Jesus Christ to God, even the Father." (Eph. 5:20)

> "In everything give thanks; for this is God's will for you in Christ Jesus." (1 Thess. 5:18)

> "Praise the Lord! Oh, give thanks to the Lord; for He is good; for His lovingkindness is everlasting." (Ps. 106:1)

This Next Week:

As we know, these are just a few of the many, many verses in the Bible about giving thanks to God for all things. Study your Bible this week and take the time to thank God for what you have and what He is about to give you. Always, in everything, give Him thanks!

Notes, special thoughts, and
prayers for my baby.

_____
_____
_____
_____
_____
_____
_____
_____
_____
_____
_____
_____
_____
_____
_____
_____
_____
_____
_____
_____
_____
_____
_____
_____
_____
_____
_____
_____

Week 39

So not much changes in these last few days except that you may really feel a drop of your baby's head into the pelvis area as it is getting ready for its exit. If you're not sure about this, your doctor will confirm placement of the baby and if he or she is ready and in the right position. All systems are go!

There's something very interesting about the feeling of knowing something really big is about to happen but you don't know when. Kind of makes it really exciting though, doesn't it? As I said, I was induced at exactly thirty-nine weeks to the day, and three days later, my son was born. Yes, you read that right, I labored for three days. Not terrible painful labor, but labor nonetheless. Just being in the hospital for four nights was the worst part! I'm not telling you this to worry you, but it's real life and that's how things sometimes go.

If you would ask me now if I would pick the same situation, no, I may not have dreamed of having my child over such a drawn-out period, but you know what? That's our story, and I'm sticking with it! My son arrived safe and sound at the end of the day, and by 10:45 p.m., I was holding my baby boy in my arms. My story may not sound appealing to the masses, but for reasons I now see, that's how it happened, and I love it.

What do the Scriptures say?

Thinking about the time it took to have my son and the weariness at the time and just being plain tired from being big and pregnant, I look back and I am amazed at what my body did and the strength I had to go through it. God provided what I needed to endure that time and He will for you as well.

In Isaiah 40:29 it says, "He gives strength to the weary, and to him who lacks might He increases power."

This Next Week:

Remember this verse at this time and carry it with you. You will be given the right amount of strength you will need just at the right time. God made our bodies to be able to do this and you are no different. Be strong in the Lord and know that He will give you the physical strength to do this!

Notes, special thoughts, and prayers for my baby.

Week 40

*I*f you are still with me, and still reading along, then you may have made it all the way to the fortieth week. You made it to the final, final finish line, girl! Lucky for you, your prize is coming any moment, or with any luck, you are holding your precious, beautiful babe in your arms this very moment.

What do the Scriptures say?

Psalm 127:3 says, "Behold, children are a gift from the Lord; the fruit of the womb is a reward."

I pray for you that you have happily received your special little miracle from God. You and your partner have studied the Word of God on how to purify your lives and be united as a family, have the Lord dwell within your home, how to train your child in the ways of the Lord, and ultimately to lead them to Christ.

You will be amazing parents, with a God-centered home where your child and future children will grow up seeing you as Godly role models. Always hold steadfast to the promises God has given us in His Word. Train up your children.

I leave you with this last passage of Scripture from Psalm 128:1–5. Blessedness of the fear of the Lord. "How blessed is everyone who fears the Lord, who walks in His ways. When you shall eat of the fruit of your hands, you will be happy, and it will be well with you. Your wife shall be like a fruitful vine, within your house, your children like olive plants around your table. Behold, for thus shall the man be blessed who fears the Lord."

Congratulations and God bless you!

Notes, special thoughts, and
prayers for my baby.

About the Author

Candace Michel was born and raised in British Columbia, Canada, where she worked as an Interior Designer until 2010, when she married her husband, Robert, and moved to Washington State. They now reside in Arlington, Washington, with their three-year-old son, Judah, on a forty-acre horse ranch. Candace's greatest joy is caring for her family, a few four-legged animals, and serving the community where they live.

CPSIA information can be obtained
at www.ICGtesting.com
Printed in the USA
BVHW081123211221
624584BV00008B/444